SALES MAVEN

SELL LIKE A GIRL

The Modern Saleswoman's Handguide

BY AMANDA LEE

ISBN 9798874018825

TABLE OF CONTENTS

INTRODUCTION

Congratulations! You've chosen a career in the exciting world of Sales, where success is only limited by your perseverance and adaptability…and occasionally, the patriarchy.

With two decades as a Sales Professional, I've journeyed through diverse industries, facing unique challenges, all within the backdrop of predominantly male-centric domains.

In the early chapters of my career, the gender imbalances were glaring, and my learning curve extended beyond sales techniques; it was about survival in a market crafted by and for men. Through swift and, at times, harsh lessons, I adapted, advancing with each challenge. Now, in this ever-evolving marketplace, I stand as a testament to the boundless adaptability inherent in every woman. Adaptability and perseverance just a few of are our greatest assets, and you will need them in Sales.

Within the pages of this book, I extend an invitation to embark on a transformative journey. I'll impart the invaluable lessons gleaned from my experiences, share the strategies that proved effective, and illuminate the mindset that has shaped me into a successful, Saleswoman in a modern era *without* a college degree. I'm not advocating against education; I am simply proving that a path exists for all who desire a career in Sales. Whether you're at the inception of your career or aiming to elevate your existing sales prowess, this book serves as a guide—a compass steering you toward the essential tools, insights, and inspiration needed to navigate the intricacies of today's business landscape. Unlock your full potential and emerge as a formidable force in the world of Sales. Welcome to a new chapter of success.

CHAPTER 1: PERSONAL BRAND

What is Your Personal Brand?

In today's marketplace, everyone is trying to sell something; standing out from the crowd is essential. Your personal brand is the unique combination of your skills, values, personality traits, and reputation that sets you apart from others in the industry. It is the impression you leave on people's minds when they interact with you or hear about you. To begin harnessing the power of your personal brand, take a moment to reflect on the following questions:

What are your strengths and expertise? Identify the skills and knowledge that differentiate you from others in your field. Consider the unique value you bring to your customers and the specific areas in which you excel.

What are your core values? Your values shape your actions and decisions. They reflect who you are as an individual and as a Sales Professional. Clarify the principles that guide your work and the impact you aim to make on your customers and the industry. Begin by reflecting on your core values and what truly matters to you. Consider how these values align with your Sales career and the type of professional you aspire to be. Authenticity starts with a deep understanding of your beliefs and the unwavering commitment to staying true to them.

How do others perceive you? Ask for honest feedback from colleagues, mentors, and customers. Gain insight into how your personal brand is currently perceived and the strengths you can leverage or areas for improvement.

Assessing Your Brand's Impact

To maximize your sales potential, it is crucial to assess how your personal brand is working for you and against you. Consider the following factors:

Consistency: Is your personal brand consistent across various touchpoints, including social media profiles, emails, networking events, and client interactions? Consistency builds trust and reinforces your brand identity.

Authenticity: Is your personal brand an authentic representation of who you truly are? Authenticity fosters genuine connections with customers and enhances your credibility as a saleswoman.

Online Presence: Evaluate your online presence, including your website, social media profiles, and professional networks. Are they aligned with your personal brand? Optimize your digital footprint to showcase your expertise, share valuable content, and engage with your target audience.

Reputation: Consider your reputation within the industry and among your customers. What do people say about you when you're not in the room? Cultivate a positive reputation by consistently delivering exceptional service, demonstrating integrity, and going above and beyond to meet customer needs.

CHAPTER 2: CURATING YOUR PERSONAL BRAND

Now that you've determined your brand, let's refine it even further. Your personal brand is more than just a logo or a catchy tagline; it is the essence of who you are, what you stand for, and how you differentiate yourself from others in the competitive sales landscape. By aligning your personal brand with your values, strengths, and aspirations, you can establish a powerful presence and connect with your target audience in a meaningful way.

Your Story

Defining Your Purpose: Clarify your purpose as a saleswoman. What drives you? What impact do you want to make? Craft a compelling purpose statement that serves as a guiding light for your personal brand. This statement will anchor your actions, decisions, and interactions with others.

Telling Your Story: Develop a concise narrative that communicates your journey, experiences, and the value you bring to the table. Share your story authentically, highlighting the challenges you've overcome and the lessons you've learned along the way. Your story is a powerful tool that resonates with others and builds trust.

Engaging Your Target Audience

Understanding Your Target Audience: Gain a deep understanding of your ideal clients and their needs. Research their pain points, preferences, and aspirations. This knowledge allows you to tailor your personal brand and messaging to effectively connect with and address the unique challenges of your target audience.

Adding Value: Position yourself as a valuable resource and trusted advisor to your target audience. Share insightful content, provide educational resources, opportunities that might interest your clients. Engage in meaningful conversations. By consistently adding value, you become the go-to in your industry, enhancing your personal brand and building long-lasting relationships.

Crafting your personal brand is an ongoing process that requires self-reflection, self-awareness, and a commitment to authenticity. Embracing the power of your unique strengths, values, and story will take on various forms as you evolve in your career.

Remember, it is not about fitting into a mold; it's about standing out and being unapologetically yourself. Embrace your authenticity, and let it shine through every aspect of your sales career. By building a strong personal brand, you will attract the right clients. Your personal brand is the secret sauce that sets you apart from the competition. Embrace your uniqueness and leverage it to make a lasting impression on potential customers. If you can master these two items and utilize your personal brand effectively:

Deliver Consistent Messaging: Ensure that your personal brand messaging aligns with your sales pitch, marketing materials, and customer interactions. Consistency breeds familiarity and reinforces your brand's identity in the minds of potential customers.

Cultivate Relationships: Use your personal brand to build genuine relationships with customers. Demonstrate your expertise, provide personalized solutions, and go the extra mile to exceed their expectations. By creating meaningful connections, you establish trust and loyalty, setting the stage for long-term success, referrals, and repeat business.

CHAPTER 3: PROSPECTING

The Power of LinkedIn

In the modern world, social media platforms have become invaluable tools for sales professionals seeking to connect with prospective customers. Among these platforms, LinkedIn stands out as a powerful resource for networking and lead generation. Here are some strategies to effectively utilize LinkedIn:

Optimize Your Profile: Create a professional and engaging LinkedIn profile that showcases your personal brand, expertise, and accomplishments. Use keywords relevant to your industry to enhance discoverability. Include a compelling summary and a clear call to action. Upload a current, clear picture, dress professionally and steer clear of filters and face altering apps. You want to show prospective customers you are confident and authentic.

Build a Relevant Network: Connect with industry professionals, potential customers, and thought leaders in your field. Join relevant LinkedIn groups and engage in discussions to expand your network and establish credibility.

Share Valuable Content: Share insightful articles, industry news, and thought leadership pieces on your LinkedIn feed. Position yourself as a knowledgeable resource and engage with your connections through comments and messages.

Tapping into Instagram and Facebook – Let's Get Social!

Instagram and Facebook are not just platforms for personal connections; they also offer immense potential for sales professionals to find and engage with prospective customers.

Develop a Professional Presence: Create a separate business account on Instagram and Facebook dedicated to your sales activities. Optimize your profiles with compelling visuals, a clear description of your offerings, and relevant contact information. Showcase your brand.

Visual Storytelling: Leverage the visual nature of Instagram and Facebook to tell stories that resonate with your target audience. Share behind-the-scenes glimpses, customer success stories, and engaging content that showcases your products or services.

Engage and Build Relationships: Actively engage with your followers by responding to comments, messages, and inquiries. Be authentic, provide value, and foster meaningful connections. Join relevant Facebook groups and participate in discussions to expand your reach.

Maximize Video Conferencing and Collaboration Tools

In the modern era, face-to-face meetings are no longer restricted to physical locations. Embrace video conferencing tools like Zoom, Microsoft Teams, or Google Meet to connect with prospects regardless of their geographic location. Here's how to make the most of these technologies:

Virtual Presentations and Demos: Conduct polished virtual presentations and product demos using video conferencing tools. Prepare engaging slide decks, anticipate potential technical issues, and ensure a professional and distraction-free environment.

Webinars and Workshops: Host educational webinars and workshops to showcase your expertise and provide value to your target audience. Promote these events through your social media platforms and email campaigns to attract prospects.

Collaborative Project Management: Utilize project management tools like Trello or Asana to collaborate effectively with prospects and clients. These platforms streamline communication, ensure task accountability, and enhance the overall customer experience.

Integrating Traditional Tactics

While digital platforms and technologies are crucial, traditional tactics still hold their value in the sales process. Here are a oldies-but-goodies methods to integrate with your digital efforts:

Networking Events: Attend industry conferences, trade shows, and networking events to connect with potential customers face-to-face. These events provide opportunities to establish rapport and build relationships beyond the digital realm.

Direct Mail and Personalized Gifts: Stand out from the digital noise by sending personalized direct mail or thoughtful gifts to your prospects. A well-crafted package can leave a lasting impression and set you apart from competitors. Handwritten notes go very far in this digitized era. It's so easy to send an email with the tap of a few keystrokes, a handwritten note shows effort, thoughtfulness, and personality.

Phone Calls and Personalized Emails: Don't underestimate the power of a personal phone call or a thoughtfully crafted email. Use these methods to follow up with prospects, nurture relationships, and address any questions or concerns.

By leveraging the digital landscape and integrating traditional tactics, you can cast a wider net and creatively personalize your business strategy. Engaging with prospects on various platforms will build meaningful connections that translate into real sales.

CHAPTER 4: CONFIDENCE AND ARTICULATE COMMUNICATION

Effective communication, both written and spoken, is essential for success in sales. This chapter explores the significance of confident and articulate communication, tailored for women in sales, covering strategies for written correspondence, the art of public speaking, and building meaningful connections at work.

The Art of Public Speaking

Public speaking stands as a vital skill for any successful saleswoman, whether addressing a large audience, delivering a sales pitch, or participating in team meetings. Your capacity to communicate with confidence and clarity leaves an enduring impression.

Preparation is key so invest time in preparing your content and practicing your delivery. Familiarize yourself with the topic, structure your key points, and rehearse your presentation. The more prepared you are, the more confident you will appear.

Engage your audience. Capture attention through compelling storytelling, interactive elements, and thought-provoking questions. Use visual aids like slides or props to enhance your message and facilitate understanding.

Speak with confidence. Project confidence through body language, voice tone, and facial expressions. Maintain eye contact, stand tall, and use gestures purposefully.

Introducing Yourself

Effectively introducing yourself is pivotal for making a strong first impression and positioning yourself as a successful woman in sales. Here's how to craft an impactful self-introduction:

Be clear and concise: Craft a concise and memorable elevator pitch that communicates who you are, what you do, and the value you bring. Tailor it to reflect your personal brand and the unique aspects of your sales approach. Keep it under 30 seconds long and be ready to use it when asked what you do.

Showcase your expertise: Highlight industry knowledge, experience, and accomplishments during your introduction. Emphasize how your expertise can benefit your audience or potential customers.

Incorporate Personal Branding: Infuse your self-introduction with elements of your personal brand, conveying values, passion, and unique qualities.

Building Meaningful Connections at Work

In the sales profession, building relationships and fostering a positive work environment are key to success.

Be approachable and friendly: Display a positive attitude, a genuine smile, and an open demeanor. Introduce yourself to colleagues, show interest in their work, and actively listen during conversations.

Foster collaboration: Work with teammates on projects or initiatives, offering expertise and support. Strengthen relationships and enhance the team dynamic through effective collaboration. Don't be afraid to lead communication and reciprocate by listening effectively.

Engage in networking: Attend company events, team-building activities, industry organization Chapter Meetings and professional development workshops. Explore opportunities for networking, both within your organization and external female-centric groups. Join organizations focused on networking for women, fostering a sales sisterhood for support and mentorship.

Communication Techniques for Success

Mastering the art of public speaking, introducing yourself effectively, building relationships with colleagues, and communicating with confidence and clarity are key elements for success as a saleswoman. Here are additional communication techniques to enhance your impact:

Speak clearly and concisely. Use clear and concise language to get your message across. Avoid jargon and technical terms that may confuse your audience.

Be confident and assertive. Believe in yourself and your abilities. Use assertive language to convey your message with conviction.

Listen actively to customers, colleagues, and stakeholders. Show empathy and understanding, addressing concerns or objections with sensitivity.

By incorporating these strategies and techniques into your communication repertoire, you can navigate the challenges of the modern sales environment with confidence, building a successful and impactful career. Practice these skills, seek feedback, and continuously refine your communication abilities to thrive in the evolving sales landscape.

CHAPTER 5: DECODING THE CUSTOMER'S BUYING PROCESS

Understanding the Customer's Motivations

To become a successful saleswoman, it's crucial to investigate why, when, and how a customer chooses to buy from you. By understanding the factors that influence their decision-making process, you can tailor your approach and increase your chances of success. Here's how you can establish a framework for asking the right questions to uncover the customer's motivations:

Building Rapport and Trust: Begin by establishing a rapport with the customer. Show genuine interest in their needs, challenges, and goals. Foster trust by actively listening, empathizing, and demonstrating your expertise.

Discovering Pain Points: Probe deeper to understand the customer's pain points and challenges. Ask open-ended questions that encourage them to share their frustrations and aspirations. This will provide insights into how your products or services can address their specific needs.

Identifying Decision-Making Factors: Uncover the factors that play a role in the customer's decision-making process. Ask about their criteria for evaluating solutions, their budget considerations, and any internal stakeholders involved in the decision.

Crafting the Right Questions

As a successful saleswoman, your ability to ask the right questions is paramount. Here are some key questions to include in your toolkit:
1.   What are your specific challenges or pain points that you're looking to address?
2.   How does your current situation or process impact your business or personal goals?
3.   What are the critical factors you consider when evaluating potential solutions?
4.   Are there any specific budget constraints or financial considerations we need to take into account?
5.   Who else is involved in the decision-making process, and what are their priorities?
6.   How does timing play a role in your decision-making process? Are there any specific deadlines or milestones we need to be aware of?

Section 3: Creating an Internal Flowchart for the Decision-Making Process

To streamline your sales approach and guide your interactions with potential buyers, it can be helpful to create an internal flowchart representing the decision-making process. Here's a general framework to consider:

Identifying the Need: Determine the customer's pain points and the specific problem they are trying to solve.

Evaluating Options: Understand how the customer evaluates and compares different solutions. Consider their criteria, preferences, and decision-making factors.

Overcoming Objections: Anticipate and address potential objections that may arise during the decision-making process. Prepare compelling responses to common concerns.

Presenting a Tailored Solution: Based on the customer's needs and decision-making factors, present a customized solution that aligns with their goals and objectives.

Demonstrating Value: Clearly articulate the unique value your product or service brings to the customer. Highlight how it addresses their pain points and offers tangible benefits.

Closing the Deal: Work with the customer to finalize the details, such as pricing, contract terms, and implementation timelines. Address any remaining questions or concerns.

Send a Thank You: Whether you close the deal or not, at the end of the sales cycle send your customer a sincere thank you note. Even if you are only thanking them for the opportunity, genuine gratitude is going to be remembered.

This flowchart should serve as a flexible guide rather than a rigid script. Adapt it to each customer's unique circumstances and be prepared to adjust your approach based on their feedback and evolving needs.

By investigating the customer's motivations, asking the right questions, and creating an internal flowchart, you can navigate the customer's decision-making process more effectively, increasing your chances of success as a saleswoman in the modern world.

CHAPTER 6: PAUSE, BUT DON'T STOP; OVERCOMING OBJECTIONS AND PIVOTING STRATEGIES

In the world of sales, objections are an inevitable part of the journey. They can be challenging, but they also present opportunities for growth and success. In this chapter, we will explore strategies for overcoming objections, regrouping, and pivoting as needed. We will also delve into the power of low-pressure persistence and the importance of reading the room to conduct your next move effectively.

Embracing Objections as Opportunities

Reframe Objections: Instead of viewing objections as roadblocks, see them as opportunities for deeper understanding and connection with the customer. Each objection provides valuable insight into their concerns and allows you to tailor your approach accordingly.

Active Listening: Pay close attention to the objections raised by the customer. Listen with empathy, seek clarification, and paraphrase their concerns to demonstrate understanding. This not only helps you address their objections effectively but also builds rapport and trust.

Regrouping and Pivoting Strategies

Analyze and Reflect: Take a step back when faced with objections. Analyze the situation objectively and reflect on your previous interactions. Consider whether there are any gaps in your approach, areas for improvement, or alternative strategies to explore.

Adapt and Pivot: Based on your analysis, make necessary adjustments to your sales strategy. This might involve refining your messaging, offering additional information or alternatives, or exploring new angles that resonate with the customer's objections.

The Power of Low-Pressure Persistence

Practice Patience: Successful saleswomen understand the value of patience. They know that persistence is crucial but must be balanced with sensitivity to the customer's needs and timeline. Respect their decision-making process and maintain a positive, low-pressure approach.

Follow-Up Effectively: Develop a well-planned follow-up strategy that demonstrates your commitment and dedication. Utilize various communication channels, such as emails, phone calls, and personalized messages, to stay on their radar without being pushy.

Reading the Room and Adjusting Accordingly

Nonverbal Cues: Pay attention to nonverbal cues, such as body language and facial expressions, during sales interactions. They can provide valuable insights into the customer's level of engagement, interest, or hesitations. Adjust your approach based on these cues to maintain a positive connection.

Ask for Feedback: Seek feedback from the customer after addressing their objections. This shows your commitment to understanding their needs and tailoring your solutions accordingly. Use their feedback as a learning opportunity to continuously improve your sales techniques.

Overcoming objections is not about winning an argument or pressuring the customer. It's about building trust, understanding their concerns, and providing value. By embracing objections, regrouping when necessary, persisting with low-pressure tactics, and reading the room to adjust your approach, you can navigate objections effectively and increase your chances of success as a saleswoman in the modern world.

Pause, take a breath, but don't stop. Every objection is an invitation to refine your approach and strengthen your sales skills. Embrace objections as opportunities, adapt your strategies, and persist with patience and empathy. By doing so, you will overcome objections with grace and be more successful in the long run.

CHAPTER 7: IT'S A NUMBERS GAME

To follow up on the previous chapter; remember that adaptation is everything in sales and in life. It is normal to feel disappointment from a missed sale or slow quarter, but you can't spend too much time dissecting that. It's imperative that you move on and focus your energy on the next opportunity. Adaption. Is. Everything. If you don't adapt to the evolving marketplace, attitudes, and evolving technologies, you are going to be left behind; no matter what the industry, everything requires adaption at some point. A failure or missed sale is merely the need for adaption. Sales is a dynamic and ever-changing landscape, and to succeed, you must embrace challenges head-on and with flexible thinking.

In the world of sales, setbacks and failures are inevitable. Deals may fall through, clients may reject your offers, and you may face countless obstacles along the way. However, it's crucial to view these challenges as valuable learning opportunities. Instead of dwelling on misgivings or allowing failures to dampen your spirit, approach them with a growth mindset. Analyze what went wrong, identify areas for improvement, and use these experiences as steppingstones towards personal and professional growth.

It's important not to take these setbacks personally. Remember, Sales is a numbers game, and not every prospect will convert into a customer. Develop a thick skin and maintain a sense of objectivity. By separating your self-worth from the outcomes of your sales efforts, you can focus on refining your approach, adapting to feedback, and persevering with resilience.

When faced with a setback, take the time to regroup and recalibrate. Reflect on your sales strategies, evaluate your target market, and identify potential gaps or areas of improvement.

Keeping your sales pipeline full of prospects is essential for sustainable success. Continuously seek out new opportunities to connect with potential clients and nurture relationships to ensure a steady flow of prospects. In a numbers game, the more you have in the pipeline, the better your odds one of them closes

CHAPTER 8: NETWORKING FOR REAL

Although we are in a modern business market, one tenet has remained constant in sales: networking is a major, if not the most important cornerstone for success. This chapter explores effective strategies for modern women in sales, covering associations and organizations, board involvement, reputation-building, authentic relationship cultivation, setting sales goals, and preparing your own mindset for success.

Research Industry-Relevant Associations

When navigating the professional landscape, aligning yourself with industry-relevant associations proves instrumental. Dive deep into their mission, values, and member benefits to gauge compatibility with your aspirations. Explore testimonials and success stories to understand the real impact of these associations. Prioritize attendance at events hosted by relevant associations, armed with a concise elevator pitch and a strategic approach to engaging with industry leaders.

Joining the Board: Maximizing Influence

Volunteer for Committees: To truly maximize your influence, identify committees that resonate with your expertise and interests. Showcase initiative by volunteering for specific projects, collaborating with committee members to build rapport, and eventually leading or significantly contributing to committee initiatives. This involvement becomes a platform for expressing innovative ideas and solutions.

Seek Leadership Opportunities: Before pursuing leadership roles, establish a strong presence within the association. Express your interest, understand the requirements, and articulate your vision for contributing to the association's success. Networking with current board members is crucial for gaining support and positioning yourself as a candidate.

Building Your Reputation

Share Your Expertise: Become a thought leader by contributing content that showcases your knowledge. Leverage platforms like LinkedIn and industry-specific forums to disseminate your insights. Explore speaking opportunities at conferences or webinars and collaborate with other thought leaders on joint projects.

Leverage social media: Develop a content strategy aligned with your personal brand and industry interests. Actively engage with peers, industry influencers, and potential clients on social media. Participate in relevant discussions to expand your network and monitor analytics to understand what resonates with your audience.

Cultivating Authentic Relationships

Be Genuine and Supportive: Approach networking with sincerity, actively listening, and offering support. Share relevant resources and celebrate the successes of your network genuinely. Foster collaboration by being open to sharing your experiences and insights.

Follow Up and nurture connections: Craft personalized follow-up messages after networking events, expressing gratitude, and reiterating your interest in collaboration. Schedule follow-up meetings or calls to explore potential opportunities and maintain relationships over time.

Setting and Attaining Sales Goals with an Abundance Mindset

Define Your Vision: Articulate your aspirations and long-term impact within your sales career. Seek feedback to ensure alignment with industry expectations and regularly review and refine your vision.

SMART Goals: Break down long-term goals into smaller, specific objectives using the SMART framework. Develop a timeline, share your goals for accountability, and regularly evaluate and adjust them.

Attaining Your Goals and Overcoming Setbacks: Develop detailed action plans, prioritize tasks, and cultivate a persistent mindset. Seek feedback to overcome challenges and adapt strategies based on the evolving landscape.

Mini-Goals and Staying on Track: Identify key milestones, celebrate achievements, and regularly review progress. Share your successes with your network, using mini goals as opportunities for reflection.

Evaluating and Refining Your Goals: Schedule regular goal evaluation sessions, seek diverse feedback, and be open to refining goals based on changing dynamics. Consider external factors, document lessons learned, and use them to inform future planning.

Embracing an Abundance Mindset: Cultivate a mindset embracing the abundance of opportunities. Surround yourself with positive influences and mentors, seek learning opportunities, and regularly express gratitude for the encountered possibilities.

Setting and attaining sales goals is an ongoing process requiring dedication, perseverance, and adaptability. Embrace the journey, celebrate successes, and learn from setbacks. With an abundance mindset, approach goals with confidence, attract opportunities, and create a positive impact on your sales career.

CHAPTER 9: NAVIGATING A TOXIC INDUSTRY; ESTABLISHING BOUNDARIES AND MAINTAINING COMPOSURE

In this chapter, we will address the unique challenges faced by women in male dominated industries and provide strategies for successfully navigating such environments. We'll explore how to effectively work with male bosses and co-workers, draw professional boundaries, assert yourself, don't allow domination, and maintain grace and composure in unprofessional circumstances. The world is changing but as of 2023 when this book goes to print and we're far from equal to our male counterparts.

Male Bosses, the good, the bad and the lawsuit waiting to happen.

Communicate Clearly: Establish open and transparent communication channels with your male boss. Clearly articulate your ideas, goals, and concerns. By effectively conveying your thoughts, you demonstrate your professionalism and competence.

Seek Mentorship and Support: Seek out mentors who can provide guidance and support. A mentor can offer valuable insights into navigating the industry and help get guide you during challenges you may face.

Sexual Harassment: An unfortunate undertone that still lingers in the workplace, is sexual harassment. Luckily, there are laws that protect abuse of power and sexual harassment, and this guide is not going to do a deep dive on this subject. But I would be remiss if I wrote a sales manual for women and didn't at least acknowledge that it still exists. My advice is to be prepared for anything, don't be naïve to think it won't happen to you, be diligent and if a boundary is crossed, document everything and quickly decide on next steps. There are bad guys and good guys, and some are both. The dynamic profession of sales will present a wide array of characters to you – be ready for anything.

Establishing Professional Boundaries

Be Assertive: Assertiveness is crucial in maintaining professional boundaries. Express your thoughts and opinions confidently, without aggression or defensiveness. Assertiveness allows you to assert your presence and expertise while remaining respectful.

Set Expectations Early: Clearly communicate your expectations regarding treatment, respect, and collaboration. By setting boundaries from the outset, you establish a framework for professional interactions and create an environment that promotes mutual respect.

Overcoming Being Talked Over or Dominated

Claim Your Space: Take up physical and verbal space in conversations and meetings. Speak with confidence, maintain good posture, and make eye contact. Assert yourself as an equal participant in discussions and ensure your voice is heard.

Use Active Listening: Active listening techniques, like paraphrasing and summarizing, demonstrate your engagement and understanding.

Grace and Composure Under Pressure

Practice Emotional Intelligence: Develop emotional intelligence to navigate unprofessional circumstances gracefully. Manage your emotions effectively, respond rather than react, and maintain a professional demeanor, even in challenging situations.

Seek Support Systems: Build a strong support network of like-minded individuals who understand the unique challenges you face. Surround yourself with mentors, colleagues, or friends who can offer guidance and provide a safe space for discussing professional challenges.

Your gender should never undermine your worth or capabilities in a male-dominated industry or any industry at all. By establishing professional boundaries, asserting yourself with confidence, and maintaining grace under pressure, you can thrive and prosper in Sales. Embrace your unique perspective and contributions as a saleswoman and continue to foster an inclusive and diverse environment within your industry. Stay true to your values, focus on your strengths, and remain committed to your professional growth. With these strategies and a resilient mindset, you can navigate a career in sales, even in a male-dominated industry, with composure and success.

CHAPTER 10: EMPOWERING WOMEN IN SALES: CELEBRATING THE TRIUMPHS AND EMBRACING OUR POTENTIAL

In this final chapter, we will reflect on the lessons learned from successful businesswomen throughout history and celebrate their accomplishments. We will delve into the journeys of these remarkable women who mastered their destinies and paved the way for future generations. Additionally, we will explore the progress made by women in the sales industry, drawing on statistics that highlight the significant shift from the 1950s to the present day. Finally, we will embrace the freedoms and opportunities available to modern women, encouraging them to set their own path in sales.

Learning from Trailblazing Women

Lessons from History: Explore the stories of influential women entrepreneurs who defied societal expectations and achieved remarkable success. From Madam C.J. Walker, the first self-made female millionaire, to Estée Lauder, who built a cosmetics empire, these women overcame obstacles and left lasting legacies. At a time when women in business were scarce, trailblazers have come before you and widened the road for you and me. Research previous generations of our business foremothers, it can instill a sense of gratitude and fortitude that will motivate you in challenging times.

Mastering Destiny: Discover common themes among these women's journeys, such as resilience, determination, and an unwavering belief in themselves. Understand that each successful woman crafted her own path, defying conventions and leaving a mark on their industries. Determine what your mark will be and visualize how you will leave it.

Women in Sales: A Shift in Paradigm

Embracing the Data: Examine the statistics that showcase the progress made by women in sales. Compare the limited opportunities available to women in the 1950s to the diverse and inclusive landscape of the present day. Celebrate the growing number of women excelling in sales roles and recognize the positive impact they have made. From women you know to public figures, inspiring women abound.

Attitude of Gratitude: Reflect on the freedom and opportunities modern women enjoy in the workplace. From the right to vote to the advancements in gender equality legislation, recognize the pivotal moments that have allowed women to thrive in sales and other professional fields. Do not take the progress built on the backs of our mothers and grandmothers for granted.

Unlocking Your Potential

Set Your Path: Embrace the potential within you as a modern saleswoman. Recognize the freedom you have to shape your own career and destiny. Develop a strong sense of purpose and seize the opportunities available to you in the sales industry.

Focus on the Positive: Maintain a positive mindset as a foundation for embracing your full potential. Acknowledge achievements, no matter how small, and celebrate successes along your journey. Positive thinking enhances resilience, fosters creativity, and contributes to a constructive work environment.

Practice Self-Compassion: Be kind to yourself and recognize that everyone encounters challenges. Practice self-compassion by treating yourself with the same kindness and understanding you extend to others. Embrace a growth mindset, viewing mistakes as opportunities to learn and improve.

Affirmations and Visualization: Incorporate positive affirmations and visualization techniques into your daily routine. Affirmations reinforce a positive self-image and mindset, while visualization helps you picture and manifest your desired outcomes.

These practices contribute to building confidence and reinforcing your belief in your potential. Embracing your potential involves fostering resilience, innovation, cultivating a positive mindset, and navigating the unique challenges of the sales landscape. By incorporating these elements, you empower yourself to unlock your full potential as a modern saleswoman.

EMBRACE YOUR JOURNEY

As we conclude this book, remember that you are part of a lineage of strong, determined saleswomen who have paved the way for your success. Learn from the lessons of history and the experiences of those who came before you. Recognize the progress made by women in sales and leverage the freedoms and opportunities available to you in the modern world. There's a lot of money to be made in sales, commission based or salaried commission; there are so many ways to control your own financial destiny if you're willing to work hard and follow your process intuitively. Don't undermine yourself.

Empowerment begins with believing in yourself and your abilities. Embrace the challenges and triumphs that lie ahead and celebrate the unique strengths and perspectives you bring to the sales industry. Remember, you have the power to set your own path, shape your own destiny, and achieve greatness as a successful saleswoman in the modern world.

Go forth and sell like a girl, Sales Maven.

Dear Reader,

In writing this book, my aim was to create a resource that can be universally beneficial to individuals from all walks of life, with a particular focus on a guide to help women in sales. I believe that the topics and insights explored within these pages hold the potential to empower and inspire saleswomen in their unique journeys. My intention is to foster personal growth, encourage self-belief, and provide guidance that can even transcend gender boundaries. I appreciate and value the diversity of all readers, recognizing that each person's experience is unique and equally important. I hope this book serves as a source of support, motivation, and wisdom for all who turn its pages…but, to my sales sisters in the trenches, this one's for you.

Amanda Lee

AUTHOR BIO

Amanda Lee is a Senior Technical Sales Professional with over 20 years of experience in technical sales and team management, successfully closing millions of dollars in sales and exceeding quotas year over year in both domestic and international products. As a proven sales expert, she has been recruited by some of the largest tech, real estate, and consulting firms in the country to build sales teams and mentor the next generation of sales leaders. She has traveled extensively throughout the United States and Canada, negotiating corporate agreements, multi-year contracts, government, and international sales. Alongside her professional achievements, Amanda is a dedicated mother, activist, and women's advocate. Based in California, she volunteers her time at women's shelters and philanthropic agencies that support and empower women in various aspects of their lives, including career coaching and preparation for entry into the workforce. Amanda's forthcoming book, "Sales Maven," draws from her expertise and experiences, providing practical strategies and inspiration that apply to any industry for a woman seeking success in sales.

Amanda draws her sales expertise from 20+ years of sales consulting in the following industries:

Pharmaceutical
Ad Marketing Sales
Corporate Staffing and Recruitment Sales
Sub-Prime Auto-Financing Sales
Real Estate
Clinical and Environmental Laboratory Sales
Environmental Consulting
Government RFQ Procurement and Contracting

Write it down! Extra pages are included intentionally for the reader to jot down themes that resonate.